YOU CHOOSE
BOOKS ™

AT BATTLE IN
WORLD WAR II

AN INTERACTIVE BATTLEFIELD ADVENTURE

D1297229

by Matt Doeden

Consultant:
Dennis P. Mroczkowski
Colonel, U.S. Marine Corps Reserve (Retired)
Williamsburg, Virginia

CAPSTONE PRESS
a capstone imprint

You Choose Books are published by Capstone Press,
1710 Roe Crest Drive, North Mankato, Minnesota 56003
www.capstonepub.com

Library of Congress Cataloging-in-Publication Data
Doeden, Matt.
  At battle in World War II : an interactive battlefield adventure / by Matt Doeden.
    pages cm. — (You choose books. You choose: battlefields)
  Includes bibliographical references and index.
  Summary: "In You Choose format, explores the technology and tactics
of World War II"—Provided by publisher.
  Audience: Grades 4–6.
  ISBN 978-1-4914-2152-9 (library binding)
  ISBN 978-1-4914-2394-3 (paperback)
  ISBN 978-1-4914-2398-1 (eBook PDF)
1. World War, 1939–1945—Juvenile literature. 2. Plot-your-own stories. I. Title.
  D743.7.D63 2015
  940.54—dc23   2014024320

Editorial Credits
Mari Bolte, editor; Tracy Davies McCabe and Charmaine Whitman, designers;
Wanda Winch, media researcher; Laura Manthe, production specialist

Photo Credits
Capstone, 44; CriaImages.com: Jay Robert Nash Collection, 12; Getty Images:
Keystone, 20, Mondadori Portfolio, 10, 26, 31, Sovfoto/UIG, 37; Newscom: akg-
images, 61, 76, akg-images/Ernst Voller, 102, DPA/picture-alliance, 55, Everett
Collection, 105; Rick Reeves: rickreevesstudio.com, cover; Shutterstock: Keith
Tarrier, 89; Superstock: Prisma, 17; U.S. Army, 6, Boyle, 47, Braun, 40; Franklin, 52,
Hendrickson, 84, Klosterman, 43, OWI, 59; U.S. Coast Guard, 71; U.S. Marine Corps:
Lt. David D. Duncan, 78, S.Sgt. Walter F. Kleine, 97; U.S. Naval History and Heritage
Command, 101; U.S. Navy photo, 68

Printed in Canada.
092014   008478FRS15

TABLE OF CONTENTS

4

ABOUT YOUR ADVENTURE

YOU are fighting in World War II (1939–1945). It is an epic battle between powerful armies and navies across the world. New weapons and technology have made this unlike any war ever fought. Fleets of airplanes, giant warships, and armored tanks dominate the battlefield. Soldiers carry weapons that fire faster, farther, and more accurately than ever before.

What choices will you make on the battlefield, with your life and the lives of your fellow fighters on the line? Can you survive and triumph in one of the biggest wars ever fought?

YOU CHOOSE the path you take through history.

An estimated 15 million soldiers from around the world died fighting in World War II. Another 25 million were wounded.

A WORLD AT WAR

War rages around the globe. On one side are the Allied forces—the United States, Great Britain, France, the Soviet Union, China, and other countries that fight with them. On the other side are the Axis nations—Germany, Italy, Japan, and the countries that support them.

From the blue waters of the Pacific Ocean to the muddy trenches of central Europe, millions are fighting battles that will decide the future of the world. It's been called the War of the Nations and the Great Patriotic War but most commonly the Second World War or World War II.

Turn the page.

In Europe, German leader Adolf Hitler wants to conquer the continent. He and his Nazi Party are committing terrible acts in Germany, Poland, and other nations under their control.

In Asia, Japan is on its own mission of conquest. Japan's attack on the American naval base at Pearl Harbor in Hawaii has opened a new chapter in history. Now the war is being fought on two fronts.

The battlefields are filled with new weapons and technology. Powerful machine guns can fire hundreds of rounds a minute. Heavy tanks roll over everything in their paths. In the sky fighter planes engage in high-speed dogfights. Destroyers, aircraft carriers, and other warships battle for control of the oceans.

Danger lurks everywhere. In the Soviet Union, soldiers try desperately to hold back the 1942 German invasion in the Battle of Stalingrad. In 1944 Allied troops in the deep woods of Belgium try to fight off a surprise attack in the Battle of the Bulge. And the final battle of the war in the Pacific, the Battle of Okinawa, is being fought between U.S. and Japanese forces in 1945.

Every battle hangs in the balance. Where will you choose to fight?

To experience the Battle of Stalingrad as an infantryman or tank crewman, turn to page 11.

To try to hold the Allied line in the Battle of the Bulge, turn to page 41.

To take control of a U.S. Navy fighter plane during the early stages of the Battle of Okinawa, turn to page 69.

The Battle of Stalingrad dragged on for six bloody months.

2

THE BATTLE OF STALINGRAD

Thick black smoke hangs over the ruined city of Stalingrad in the Soviet Union. The city was once a proud symbol named for the nation's leader, Josef Stalin. But now it is little more than a pile of smoking rubble.

It's late 1942. For months Germany and the Soviet Union have fought over this city. It's been a bloody battle. German leader Adolf Hitler believes that victory here will break the Soviet army and drive them out of the war. The famed German 6th Army has 250,000 men, compared to the Soviet's 20,000. The Germans are better trained, better equipped, and better supported.

Turn the page.

The German 4th Air Fleet was a dominant flying force over Stalingrad.

The sound of an airplane overhead breaks the silence. You don't even have to look up to know that it's German. The German air force, known as the Luftwaffe, is the most powerful in Europe. Their fighters rule the sky. They bomb the city at will and gather intelligence on the location and movements of Soviet troops.

The German bombs have destroyed the city. Any wooden buildings were instantly demolished. The rest of the city is full of empty buildings and piles of rubble. More than 40,000 civilians have already lost their lives.

It seems the Germans have every advantage. And yet the battle for the ruined city rages on. Every collapsed building and cratered road becomes a place for the enemy to hide behind. The Soviet forces are stalling for time. Help is coming, if only they can hold out long enough.

To fight with the German 6th Army inside the city of Stalingrad, turn to page 14.

To join a Soviet tank unit preparing to attack German lines north of the city, turn to page 16.

Stalingrad is your worst nightmare. As a member of Germany's famed 6th Army, you've known nothing but success so far in the war. But your tactics, which have been unstoppable on open fields of battle, are worthless inside the tangled rubble of the city. It seems everything you know about warfare is wrong.

You creep along the outer edge of an apartment building. Around the corner you see the banks of the Volga River. The river is the key to the city. The Soviets are desperate to control it. They can't supply their troops without it.

Gunfire rattles in one of the upper floors of the building. Your commander has ordered your unit to take control of it. But that won't be easy. The Soviets have dug in deep, and you'll have to fight for every inch.

You've got your trusty G41 semiautomatic rifle over your shoulder, as well as a few hand grenades clipped to your belt. You're ready for a fight.

The open frame of the building's front door looms ahead. The door itself has been blasted away. You can see scorched pieces lying on the ground. It's time to go inside.

To throw a grenade into the doorway before you enter, turn to page 18.

To charge in with your rifle at the ready, turn to page 20.

"They're calling it Operation Uranus," says Sergei, your commanding officer. Over his shoulder, you can see the smoldering ruins of Stalingrad.

"Germany has put all of its strength into the city," Sergei continues. "Hitler has placed weaker, poorly equipped Romanian troops farther north. We will break through this line and circle back. A second attack will break through south of the city. When we meet up, we'll have the Germans surrounded."

The attack is about to begin. You're in command of a Soviet T-34 tank. It's a powerful fighting machine with heavy armor, dangerous weapons, and a sturdy engine.

The command comes: "Attack!" Hundreds of tanks rumble together over uneven ground toward the enemy line.

Hitler forbade the 6th Army from surrendering. He expected them to fight to the last man.

The enemy responds with artillery fire. Just 20 feet from you, the ground erupts. An artillery shell tears apart the tank next to you. You see shreds of red, yellow, and green fabric floating in the air. Those colored flags were used to signal orders from your company commander.

You swallow. Your commander is either dead or seriously injured. You're on your own.

"Orders?" asks Georgy, the T-34's driver.

To continue moving toward the enemy line, turn to page 22.

To fall back and return fire, turn to page 23.

The members of the German 6th Army learned quickly that a grenade is a soldier's best friend. The stick-shaped grenade feels familiar in your hand. You use your other hand to pull the string that lights the grenade's fuse. Then you lob it through the doorway.

BOOM!

You step into a dark hallway filled with swirling dust. You hear groans to your right. When your eyes adjust to the darkness, you see two Soviet soldiers on the ground. You raise your rifle and squeeze off two quick shots to finish the job.

You move carefully through the building. You find no more Soviet troops on the first floor, so you slowly climb a stairwell to the second. As soon as you reach the second floor landing, shots ring out.

You duck back behind the corner, gripping your rifle. When you hear footsteps, you swing back out into the hallway and open fire. The enemy spots you too late, and he drops to the floor.

Two more soldiers rush out, catching you by surprise. One lunges at you with a sharp bayonet attached to a rifle. But you manage to dodge the attack. You bring the butt of your own rifle down onto his head. Then you spin and raise your rifle toward the second man. He stands there with his own rifle raised. Slowly he lifts one hand, palm spread. He takes a small step back.

19

"No shoot," he says in broken German.

The man seems to be offering a truce.

To shoot him anyway, turn to page 28.

To raise your own hand and agree to a truce, turn to page 29.

Stalingrad was also called the Rat's War because both sides fought in the streets for every available inch of space.

You'll save your hand grenades for later, when you know there's an enemy in wait. You creep along the building quietly until you're just outside the door. As quickly as you can, you dive in through the doorway, your G41 raised and ready to fire.

It takes a moment before your eyes adjust to the darkness. But that's too long. The enemy opens fire. You hear bullets ping off of a wall behind you. Without thinking, you raise your rifle and send off a few blind shots in return. You don't expect to hit anyone, but it should buy you a few precious seconds.

A quick glance shows a hallway stretching the length of the building in each direction. Open doors line the hallway on both sides. You know the shot came from your right, but you have no idea exactly where the shooter is positioned.

To dive left through one of the open doorways, turn to page 25.

To charge right in hopes of taking the shooter before he can alert others, turn to page 33.

"Keep it rolling," you order. Your mission is to break through the enemy line, not set up for a long battle. The Romanian troops aren't well trained or equipped. Their artillery is old and outdated. Yet they're dug into their position, and they're ready to defend it. A large antitank battery sits at the frontline. If you could target and destroy it, it would make the approach much easier. But the enemy fire grows more intense with every second.

"All of the other tanks are falling back," Georgy reports. "That must be the order."

22

You're almost in range. Another few feet and you could take out some of the enemy artillery.

To fall back with the other tanks, go to page 23.

To try to take your shot at the enemy artillery, turn to page 31.

The Romanians may have outdated artillery. But they'll hit you hard with what they have.

"Fall back," you tell Georgy. Another blast hits the ground a few dozen feet ahead of you as Georgy backs the T-34 away.

You're not alone. The rest of your unit is doing the same thing. You decide to regroup for another strike.

Your next attack is repelled as well. But you keep trying. Finally, around noon, a third attack succeeds. Your unit is right on the front lines, and this time the enemy doesn't have the firepower to send you back.

Enemy soldiers fire at your tank with their rifles. But the T-34 has strong armor. You smile as you hear the *ting, ting, ting* of bullets bouncing harmlessly off the tank.

Turn the page.

Your T-34 rolls effortlessly over Romanian and German artillery, destroying everything in its path.

Most of the tanks in your unit are blasting through the hole in the enemy's line straight ahead. But just to the north, you spot the enemy attempting to regroup near an artillery battery.

24

To follow your unit and attack the main line, turn to page 36.

To attack the regrouping enemies, turn to page 38.

You quickly dart to your left, hopping over a pile of crushed cinder blocks and through an open doorway. You roll and spring to your feet, rifle ready to fire. But the room is empty.

Outside, shots echo through the hallway. You hear two voices shouting in Russian. You hold your breath and remain as still as you can, not wanting to give up your position.

A few minutes later, you hear footsteps. You quietly grab a grenade, pull the pin, and throw it down the hallway. You turn and cover your ears just in time. *BOOM!* The building shakes. Dust fills the air. Then all is silent.

Carefully, you peek out the door. In the rubble, you see several Soviet soldiers lying on the ground.

To continue your sweep of the building, turn to page 26.

To check the bodies to see if they have any useful weapons, turn to page 30.

You move as quietly as you can down the hall, toward a stairwell. Over the next hour, you move carefully from room to room. You take one enemy soldier by surprise, slashing his throat with your knife. The next one sees you coming. You duck behind a wall as he opens fire. The bullets ping off the concrete walls, but a well-thrown grenade puts an end to the attack.

Fighting in a rubble-filled city was something the German 6th Army had never experienced before.

Finally you clear the last room. The soldier inside is a sniper. His gaze is so fixed outside his window that he never saw you coming.

"The building is clear," you radio back after confirming the sniper is dead. Then you sink to the floor. Your nerves are shot. This type of warfare is brutal and exhausting. You can't wait to be done with it. But there's a long way to go, and every inch is a battle.

Turn to page 34.

You shake your head and squeeze the trigger of your rifle. You take no pleasure in the killing, but you're no fool. The man would probably have killed you the moment you lowered your weapon. And if not, then he had no business being a soldier in the first place.

You continue your sweep of the building. You find only one more enemy soldier, a sniper who is so intent on his work that he never even sees you coming. The building is clear. It's now under German control—at least until the Soviets decide to send forces to take it back.

28

You've survived this mission. But you know the battle is far from over.

Turn to page 34.

You're tired of this dirty, messy brand of war. Suddenly the figure before you seems more like a man than an enemy. You don't want to kill him.

With a nod, you lower your weapon. You remove your left hand and lift it in the air. You may have to kill this man tomorrow, but you feel good about letting him live today.

The Soviet soldier smiles broadly. You smile back and wave a little.

Then he raises his rifle and shoots you right in the head.

THE END

To follow another path, turn to page 9.

To read the conclusion, turn to page 103.

You creep down the hallway as quietly as you can. But your boots crunch bits of concrete and debris with every step. Two bodies lie on the ground, covered in dust from the explosion.

You kick the first body. It's limp. You inch closer to the second one. The soldier's uniform is covered in blood. As you check the body for weapons, you hear a soft click.

The first soldier was killed in the blast. But you realize a split second too late that the second one is still alive. He's bloody and bruised, but that doesn't stop him from pointing a small handgun at your head.

Your enemy growls a single word in Russian. You don't understand what he said, but it's the last word you'll ever hear.

THE END

To follow another path, turn to page 9.

To read the conclusion, turn to page 103.

You're so close. Just a few seconds more and you'll be in range. "Press forward," you command. "Prepare to fire!"

The high-pitched sound of a bomber streaking through the air cuts off your command. Then a huge blast rocks your tank. The T-34 lurches and comes to a stop.

"Got the engine," Georgy tells you. "We're not going anywhere."

The German Luftwaffe dropped more than 1,000 tons of bombs over Stalingrad.

Turn the page.

Your best hope is that you and the crew can wait it out inside the tank until the next attack comes. But it's not much of a hope. You're directly in the sights of the Romanian artillery now. And there are always more bombers. Another blast will be coming any moment. And then another. And another. The T-34 is a strong tank, but it's not invincible.

You and Georgy exchange a look, knowing your lives are now measured in seconds rather than years.

"It's been an honor serving with you," Georgy says, saluting.

32

THE END

To follow another path, turn to page 9.

To read the conclusion, turn to page 103.

You spin and dart right. Your G41 rattles in your hands as you squeeze the trigger. The powerful semiautomatic rifle sprays bullets down the dark hallway.

Suddenly you spot movement. Two enemy soldiers peer around a corner ahead. You take cover behind a pile of rubble as one of them fires. You recognize the sound of an SVT-40, one of the best Soviet-issued rifles. Bad news for you.

You have to act fast. You charge at the shooter, keeping low to the ground. He fires a shot that catches you in the shoulder. But you barrel into him. Both of you fall to the floor. You lift your rifle to bring it down on your enemy's head.

That's when the second soldier fires. He saves his partner's life and ends yours.

THE END

To follow another path, turn to page 9.

To read the conclusion, turn to page 103.

The days stretch into weeks as you and the 6th Army try to capture Stalingrad. But while you do your part, the German forces outside are failing. The Soviet troops break through the German lines both north and south of the city. The main army recommends you fall back. 6th Army leaders refuse.

As the brutal cold of winter really sets in, the 6th Army is surrounded and cut off. Life is miserable. The Soviet army continues to close the gap. All the 6th Army can do is fall back. Food grows scarce. Your daily rations include old horsemeat and rats. Your clothes can't keep out the cold. It's impossible to sleep.

You and your fellow soldiers grow thin and weak. Your ammunition is almost gone. The Soviets demand you surrender. The officer in charge refuses.

When the Soviet troops storm the city in late January, you are too tired to resist. You are beaten. After the surrender the Soviets gather what German troops remain. You will march to a prison camp, they tell you.

Soviet prison camps are brutal places. You survived the bloodiest battle of World War II. But you know it's unlikely that you'll live to see the end of the war.

THE END

To follow another path, turn to page 9.

To read the conclusion, turn to page 103.

Your mission is clear: break through the enemy line. "Straight ahead," you order. The Romanian troops are in chaos ahead. Smoke hangs over the battlefield as the Soviet artillery batters the enemy.

You've done it! And the news only gets better. The attack south of Stalingrad has also succeeded. That means you've got the city surrounded.

The battle drags on for more than a month. But the German army is doomed. Their supply lines are broken, and they're unprepared for the bitter cold of winter. In early February you proudly command your T-34 to the outskirts of the city. Soon the news spreads through your camp—the Germans have surrendered.

"The tides have turned," Georgy says, shaking your hand and clapping your back in celebration. "This is the battle that will finish Hitler."

Georgy is right. The Germans never fully recover from their defeat at Stalingrad. And you were a big part of that pivotal battle.

THE END

On February 2, 1943, the Germans surrendered at Stalingrad.

To follow another path, turn to page 9.

To read the conclusion, turn to page 103.

You don't want to give the enemy any chance to regroup. "To that battery!" you order. Georgy turns the tank north and rolls toward the massing Romanian troops. Meanwhile, the ground shakes as Soviet artillery drills the enemy line. Enemy troops scatter in panic. Some come within 100 feet of your tank.

That's too close. The enemy line may be in chaos, but many of the Romanian soldiers are armed, and they continue to fight. Some open fire on your tank. Their bullets are harmless against your tank's armor. But then a few start lobbing grenades. A well-placed grenade explodes near your engine, badly damaging it.

A few more grenades and your tank is finished. The enemy swarms around you. You're overrun.

"Fight!" you order. But it's too late. You hear the T-34's hatch opening, then the *clink* of a grenade dropping onto the floor. It's the sound no tank commander ever wants to hear.

The day is victorious for the Soviets. You and your team are just a few more casualties in the bloody battle of Stalingrad.

THE END

To follow another path, turn to page 9.

To read the conclusion, turn to page 103.

American soldiers fought through blowing snow and bitterly cold temperatures during the Battle of the Bulge.

3
BATTLE OF THE BULGE

You shiver as the wind whips through the trees. Snow blows everywhere. It's cold and you can barely feel your toes. But you hold your position, knowing that German troops could fire on you at any moment.

It's December 1944 and you're in Belgium's Ardennes Forest. Allied forces have driven the German army back to their own border. But Hitler and the Germans have finally pushed back. German tanks rumble over the bumpy, heavily wooded ground. Allied soldiers—mostly Americans like yourself—are spread out, often fighting out of small foxholes.

Turn the page.

You are a member of the 101st Airborne Division. It's one of the U.S. Army's elite fighting units. You've been ordered to keep the town of Bastogne out of German hands. Several major roads converge in Bastogne. If the Germans take control, they'll be able to move that much faster as they continue to attack the Allied line.

The 101st is a tough division. But you and your fellow soldiers are low on food and ammunition. The winter is brutally cold, and many are suffering from frostbite. And if that's not enough, you're completely surrounded and badly outnumbered.

"The Germans are throwing everything they have into this offensive," says your commander, General Anthony McAuliffe. "They have a quarter of a million troops and more tanks than we can count. If we can hold Bastogne, it will slow them down a great deal.

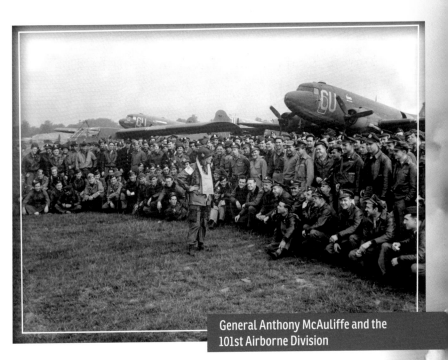

General Anthony McAuliffe and the
101st Airborne Division

McAuliffe continues, "We've spotted some German troop movement to the north. I need a scout to bring me a report. And a German Panzer division is moving in on a key crossroads to the southwest. We have to defend it."

To scout out the enemy's movements, turn to page 44.

To try to fight off the Panzer attack, turn to page 46.

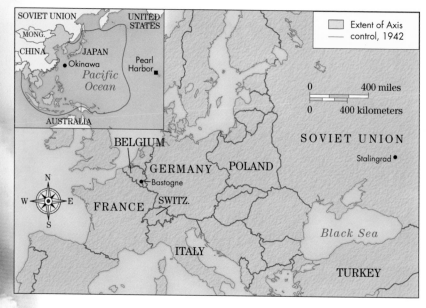

You grab your gear and head north, out of town, beyond the Allied line. Another soldier named Kenny accompanies you. The enemy watches the line closely, but with some care, you can move without being noticed.

The battlefield is covered by a fresh blanket of snow, but you can still see the shapes of dead men beneath. Many of them were your friends. You try not to think about it, staying focused on your mission.

You move along one of the major roads, staying in the trees to keep out of sight. You hear the noise of a tank coming down the road long before you see it. You dive behind a snowbank to watch.

Moments later a German Tiger I tank rumbles around a curve. The Tiger I is one of the biggest, most heavily armed tanks in the world. And it's headed straight for Bastogne's outer defenses. The tank's hatch is open, with its commander watching the road ahead. Kenny motions to a grenade and mimes throwing it.

The tank hasn't spotted you yet. Your mission is reconnaissance, not combat. "But we could be heroes!" Kenny whispers. It's just one tank. Not stopping it now could be a mistake.

To try to throw a grenade into the tank as it passes, turn to page 48.

To stay with the original mission, turn to page 63.

For much of the war, the Germans have ruled the field with their powerful Panzer tank units. The tanks have rolled over the Allied defenses, creating a large bulge in the line. Now a division of Panzer tanks is coming straight for a key crossroads near the city.

The Allied forces have dug deep trenches and foxholes near the crossroads to defend it. "Over here," shouts an officer as you approach. "We need every man we can get. I count at least 18 Panzer tanks and a battalion of infantry. We're badly outnumbered, but our line is dug in."

You scan the line. A strong artillery battery is the main defense. Twelve M1 howitzers will rain down shells on the attacking tanks. To each side of the line stand several M1917 Browning machine guns.

"We may be outnumbered," you say. "But the Germans are going to have to pay a heavy price if they want to make it through."

The M1 howitzer was also known as the Black Dragon.

To help man an M1 howitzer for the battle, turn to page 50.

To take control of one of the M1917 machine guns, turn to page 52.

It's a risky move, but a grenade tossed into the open hatch could take out the Tiger completely. It's worth the risk. You stay low behind the snow bank as the tank rolls closer and closer.

You don't dare pop your head up to take a look. So you rely just on your ears. When the tank sounds like it's right below you, you spring into action. With one motion, you grab a grenade, stand, pull the string, and pitch it gently into the tank's open hatch.

Your attack is so swift and sudden that the tank's commander doesn't have time to react. Even before he can raise his rifle, the grenade explodes with a flash of light. *BOOM!* The tank swerves sharply before grinding to a halt. The huge vehicle is now blocking the road.

The commander lies face down over the front of the tank. You see that he has dropped his rifle. Your unit is very low on ammunition. Maybe if you hurry, you could grab the rifle and some other supplies.

The explosion will draw attention quickly though. You can't afford to be captured.

To flee the scene, turn to page 54.

To try to recover some supplies, turn to page 55.

"You there," says the officer, pointing. "You know how to operate an M1?"

"Yes, sir," you answer, marching through the snow to join the other members of the gun crew.

The 75MM pack howitzer is an impressive weapon. Your job is to help prepare ammunition, set fuses, and load the huge gun.

You barely have time to introduce yourself before the fighting begins. The German Panzer tanks emerge from the woods, firing their main guns. Huge craters open up in the ground before you. It's time to return fire. Your crew expertly loads and fires several shells. The first two miss. But the third is a direct hit. The shell hits a Panzer head-on, stopping it in its tracks!

But the German infantry is still advancing. You can hear the M1917 machine guns chattering as they fire, trying to keep the Germans back. But you can tell it won't be enough. There are just too many.

To aim a shell toward the advancing infantry, turn to page 59.

To continue firing on the enemy tanks, turn to page 61.

The M1917A1 is nearly 30 years old. But it remains a force on the battlefield. You kneel down behind the tripod that mounts the heavy weapon. The gun can fire 600 rounds a minute.

As the Panzers approach, your fellow American soldiers begin firing their howitzers.

Soldiers used howitzers against tanks and aircraft.

The huge gun's shells crash down on the advancing enemy. But the Panzers have strong armor. Most keep coming. They fire their big main guns toward you, blasting huge craters in the Allied line.

Then the infantry starts its approach. You swivel your machine gun around and open fire. *Pop, pop, pop!* The weapon rattles in your hands as you cut down one enemy after the next.

But the tanks are getting too close. Over the boom of the explosions, you hear someone shouting, "Fall back!"

53

If you give up the line now, the Germans will control the crossroads.

To fall back, turn to page 57.

To continue firing, turn to page 58.

You've got critical information on German troop movements. A few rifles and some ammunition aren't worth risking for that. You take one last look at the ruined enemy tank and turn back into the cover of the forest.

You trudge through the cold and snow, shivering as the temperature begins to drop. By the time you reach base, you're shivering and can't even feel your feet. But right now, all that matters is telling your commanding officer what you've learned.

54

Turn to page 67.

The rifle is right there. There will be more weapons inside the tank. With no promise of resupply anytime soon, the 101st is in dire need of ammo. It's worth the risk, you decide.

You scramble down the bank toward the disabled tank. First you pick the rifle up off the ground. You're in luck. It's an StG 44, one of the finest assault rifles ever made. A quick check shows that it also has a full magazine of 30 rounds. You've struck a gold mine if there are more inside the tank.

The German's Tiger II tank was also called the King Tiger. It was heavily armored and weighed nearly 70 tons.

Turn the page.

You jump up and stick your head down into the hatch. The smoke and dust have begun to clear, and you see the scattered remains of the crew. But there's no time to reflect on the carnage. You carefully lower yourself inside the tank and clean out everything you can find, including two more StG 44s and more than a dozen magazines.

But as you climb out of the hatch, your heart sinks. There stand a dozen Nazi soldiers. They all wear the uniform of the SS—Hitler's elite troops. One of them shouts in heavily accented English, "Drop your weapons."

To open fire, turn to page 65.

To lower your rifle, turn to page 66.

The Allied line can't possibly hold. You're just too badly outnumbered. You turn, fire off a few final shots, then fall back with the rest of the unit.

It's a mad dash over the frozen landscape, but you soon regroup. Once again, you stand in the way of the advancing German army. This time your line holds. After a long day of fighting in the brutal cold, the enemy withdraws. You've done it. The Germans will be back, but you've at least held them off another day.

Exhausted, you and your brothers in arms return to base.

Turn to page 67.

You're not willing to give up your position. You kneel down and resume firing. Explosions rock the ground around you as you continue to mow down enemy troops. Even in the bitterly cold winter air, your gun grows hot from firing over and over again.

But in the end, it's hopeless. With no artillery to hold back the tanks, the Germans march straight toward your position. You never see the shell that finally ends your life.

Your part in the war is over. At least you took some of the enemies down with you.

58

THE END

To follow another path, turn to page 9.

To read the conclusion, turn to page 103.

American troops did all they could to slow the German army's advance.

"There!" you shout, pointing to the advancing troops. The team adjusts the angle of the weapon to fire on the advancing infantry. You release the shell. *BOOM!* Moments later, it explodes near the enemy troops. You watch as nearby tree branches shatter and fall. Several of the enemy troops are on the ground. But many more continue to advance.

Turn the page.

"Again!" you shout. But before you can get off another shot, your position comes under enemy tank fire. Dirt and snow fly around you. The explosions make your ears ring. A bullet zips past, grazing the side of your forehead and part of your ear. The Allied line is failing. Men are falling back.

You lift a hand to your forehead, and it comes back red. You're bleeding a lot. Hot, sticky blood runs into your ears and eyes, making it hard to hear and see. You feel dizzy and confused. You take off running, but you're disoriented. You don't know which direction you're heading.

That's when you run straight into a group of enemy soldiers.

To fire on the enemy soldiers, turn to page 65.

To surrender, turn to page 66.

The Tiger tank had the strongest armor and was used in head-to-head battles. The older Panzer tanks were used more for infantry support.

You have to let the machine gunners worry about the enemy troops. Your howitzer is best suited for armored targets. "There!" you shout, pointing to a Panzer. Its main gun is turning toward your position.

It's a race to see who can load faster, and your team wins. The shell slams into the front of the tank just before it can fire. Another direct hit!

Turn the page.

The battle drags on. You and your fellow soldiers continue to batter the German tanks with artillery fire. The machine guns prevent the enemy troops from marching on your position.

Eventually, the Germans' numbers force you to retreat. But you've made them pay a heavy price for that piece of ground. You and your brothers in arms return to base feeling like you've done your job.

Turn to page 67.

You shake your head. "We're supposed to be gathering information," you tell Kenny. "We need to tell General McAuliffe about this." You turn back toward the base, but Kenny doesn't follow. When you look back, you see that he has moved into the open and has his rifle raised.

"I've got a clean shot," he says. Before you can say anything, he takes the shot. The tank's heavy machine gun quickly spins around and sights your partner.

"Run!" shouts Kenny.

But there's no time. You dive low as the tank opens fire. You can hear bullets whizzing over your head as you hug the ground. You feel a blast of pain as one rips through your shoulder. Snow flies down the back of your jacket and melts, joining the cold sweat that covers your body.

63

Turn the page.

You hear the tank rumble away. You carefully make your way to what's left of Kenny. The bullet in your arm means it will be impossible to take his body with you.

You cut off Kenny's dog tags and put them in your pocket. "That will have to be enough for his family," you think as you painfully make your way back to Bastogne. You hope it won't be too late to stop the tank by the time you arrive.

THE END

To follow another path, turn to page 9.

To read the conclusion, turn to page 103.

You raise your rifle in hopes of catching the enemy by surprise. But they saw you first. Before you can take a single shot, the enemy soldiers open fire.

One bullet hits you in the leg. Another rips into your shoulder. A third catches you in the chest. But it's the one that hits you squarely in the forehead that finally ends your life.

You fought bravely for the 101st, but soon you'll be just another shape under the snow outside the town of Bastogne.

THE END

To follow another path, turn to page 9.

To read the conclusion, turn to page 103.

You have no choice. You drop your weapon and slowly place your hands on your head.

Several enemy soldiers step forward with their rifles raised. You're sure they intend to shoot you. But before they can, an officer gives an order in German. You don't understand what he said, but you're certain that he just spared your life. The soldiers scowl and lower their weapons. They grab you, seize your weapons, and shove you all the way back to the German trenches.

You're headed to a prison camp. Life there is going to make Bastogne look like a beach resort. But at least you're still alive. The war can't go on forever, and you will see home again one day.

THE END

To follow another path, turn to page 9.

To read the conclusion, turn to page 103.

"Well done, soldier," your commanding officer says after you file your report. "The Germans aren't going to stop coming for the town. But the 101st won't give them an inch of ground without a fight. Now go get some rest."

Your mission is complete, but you know there will be no real rest. Bastogne is at the heart of a massive battle, and many more will die before victory is decided. You and your fellow soldiers of the 101st are outnumbered, ill-equipped for the bitter winter, and running low on supplies. But in time, help will come. You just have to hold on until then.

THE END

To follow another path, turn to page 9.

To read the conclusion, turn to page 103.

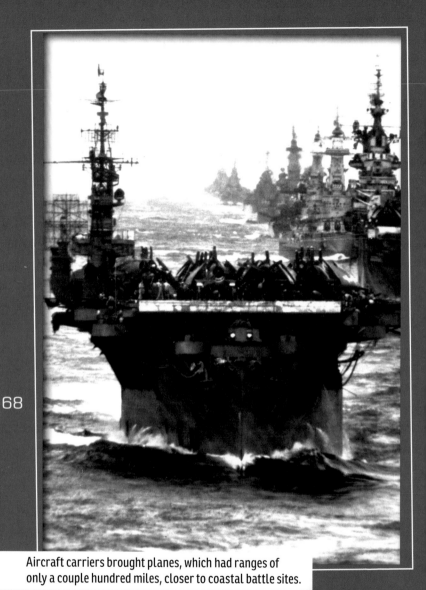

Aircraft carriers brought planes, which had ranges of only a couple hundred miles, closer to coastal battle sites.

4

THE BATTLE OF
OKINAWA

You stand on the deck of a U.S. Navy aircraft carrier. The Pacific Ocean stretches out before you, the waves lapping against the giant ship's hull. But this is no peaceful scene. All around you U.S. and British warships, tank battalions, and airplanes lie in wait. It's April 1945, and the biggest Allied invasion force of the entire war is gathering.

In the distance you can see the dark shapes of the Ryuku Islands, which form the Okinawa prefecture of Japan.

Turn the page.

Smoke rises from Okinawa, the largest of the islands, proof of the first stages of battle between Allied and Japanese forces. But the worst is yet to come. The invasion has only just begun, and the Japanese have made it clear that they plan to fight to the last man.

"It's going to be a mess out there," says your friend Gordon.

"And we're going to have a view like no other," you answer. You and Gordon are both lieutenants—and pilots—in the U.S. Navy. You trained together at the Naval Academy, and you've been together ever since. Gordon feels more like a brother than a friend.

Your mission is a go. You've just come out of a final briefing. It's a critical operation. The Allies need these islands to serve as a staging point for an invasion of the Japanese mainland.

For three and a half years, the Allies have been steadily driving the Japanese back. The war is coming to an end—a victory here could end the war. A loss will prolong the fighting.

The Allies have committed a staggering number of fighters to this invasion. More than half a million Allied forces will be involved. That's more than three times the manpower of the famous 1944 invasion of Normandy, France.

More than 1,300 U.S. ships surrounded Okinawa. It was the largest naval fleet ever gathered.

71

Turn the page.

The Japanese military is launching a desperate attack to slow the invasion. They're sending hundreds of fighter planes on a kamikaze mission. Their goal is to ram into U.S. ships in suicidal collisions. The Allies also have learned that Japan's greatest battleship, the *Yamato*, is nearing the islands.

Crews on the carrier's flight deck are busily preparing fighter planes that will join the attack on the *Yamato*. The F6F Hellcat is a dependable, battle-tested fighter plane, perfectly suited for missions based off of aircraft carriers. The F4U Corsairs are the ultimate air-to-air combat machines. They'll stay with the Allied fleet to protect it from the kamikaze attacks.

"I guess it's time," Gordon says.

To enter the battle in an F6F Hellcat, go to page 73.

To take the controls of an F4U Corsair, turn to page 75.

72

You know the controls of the F6F Hellcat like the back of your hand. It may not be the newest or flashiest fighter in the Navy, but few planes are more proven.

"The Japanese battleship *Yamato* has been spotted," says your squadron leader, Thomas. "Our intelligence says that it's on a suicide mission. The Japanese plan to run it aground near Okinawa and use its huge guns against our men on foot. We can't let that happen. A massive attack on the *Yamato* and the eight destroyers escorting it is about to begin. Our job is to keep the skies clear for our bombers."

The battle on the ground is just beginning as you approach Okinawa from the sky. Your group of Hellcats is the only thing in the air.

Where are all the enemy fighter planes?

Turn the page.

As you scan the sky, the *Yamato*'s big antiaircraft guns begin to fire. The bullets clip the wing of one of the Hellcats, sending it spiraling out of control.

"Watch out for the guns," Thomas says over the radio. "They're picking off our fighters."

"Then let's take out the guns," you answer.

"Lead the way," Thomas says, falling back.

How should you attack? You could come in with a sharp dive, using speed and surprise to your advantage. Or you could approach low, just above the waves, where you're a much harder target to hit.

74

To come in low, turn to page 82.

To build up some speed and dive in, turn to page 84.

The downfall of the Corsair is that it's a little tricky to land on an aircraft carrier. But in the air, there's nothing better. You take off and pull up and away from the carrier's flight deck.

"Check out the view," Gordon says over the radio. Now that you're in the sky, you've got a bird's-eye view of the first stages of the invasion.

From here you can see that the Allied fleet is enormous, with its aircraft carriers, destroyers, amphibious ships, and more. The troops on the ground are slowly advancing their position. You can understand why the Japanese are desperate. Their navy has been reduced to just a few ships. They have been defenseless to stop the Allies.

75

Turn the page.

Transporting troops, artillery, tanks, and other weapons by sea into enemy territory was known as amphibious warfare.

There's no time to take it all in, though. "Group of Zeros coming in, dead ahead," says Gordon over the radio. "And we've got a pair of Ki-45s coming in high."

It's time to engage. The A6M Zero is the staple of Japan's air force. They're no match for you in terms of weapons or raw speed. But they are lightning quick and their pilots seem completely fearless. Meanwhile, the larger Ki-45 could serve as a fighter or a bomber.

The Zeros appear to be headed toward an allied destroyer. They intend to ram into it. You're not sure what the Ki-45s are up to. Your Corsair is better suited to high-speed, high-altitude combat. But the Zeros are posing the more immediate threat.

"Which way?" Gordon asks.

To intercept the low-flying Zeros, turn to page 78.

To engage the high-altitude Ki-45s, turn to page 80.

"They're after that destroyer. We can't let them reach it," you say, banking your Corsair hard to meet the enemy.

You push your Corsair to the limit. It's one of the fastest planes in the sky, and easily catches the Zeros. Before long the enemy planes are within range. You open fire. Your powerful .50-caliber Browning machine guns completely shred the wing of one of the Zeros. The plane falls into a deadly spin and smashes into the ocean.

The F4U-4 Corsair could reach speeds of nearly 450 miles per hour.

But before you can celebrate, you see that Gordon is in trouble. Three enemy planes are pursuing him, and at this low altitude, he doesn't have the maneuverability he needs to get away.

"Climb!" you tell him over the radio. The Zero can't climb at the same rate as the Corsair. It's his only hope of escape.

"No way, buddy," Gordon answers. "I'm drawing these jokers off. Take care of the other two planes."

What should you do? Even though Gordon's a great pilot, you don't like his chances. But you can't let the Zeros reach the destroyer either. There's no time to think.

To get the Zeros off of Gordon's tail, turn to page 89.

To protect the destroyer, turn to page 91.

"Those Zeros will outmaneuver us down there," you say, pulling your airplane into a steep climb.

The Ki-45 pilots have spotted you as well. They're climbing still higher, trying to escape notice. But they're out of luck. You and Gordon are in pursuit, and the chase is on. The Ki-45s quickly split off in different directions.

"I've got this one," Gordon says. "Good luck."

You climb higher and higher, trying to get a shot on your Ki-45. But your enemy is a skilled pilot. He zigs and zags expertly as you continue your climb.

But you keep closing in on him. Then you've got him in your sights. You open fire. But nothing happens! Your guns must have jammed because of the colder temperatures at this height.

With no guns, how are you supposed to bring down the enemy plane?

A crazy idea pops into your head. Your Corsair has one weapon left—its big, spinning propeller blades. What if you rammed the blades right into the enemy plane? Could it work?

To attempt to ram the Ki-45 with your propeller, turn to page 93.

To give up and return to your carrier, turn to page 96.

Antiaircraft guns are designed to shoot toward the sky. The *Yamato*'s crew is going to have a hard time targeting you if you're actually below them.

You drop into a slow descent, safely out of the reach of enemy weapons. Then from just a few dozen feet above the waves, you begin to make your approach.

You watch as the big guns swing down to track you. But the enemy crew isn't used to shooting them at a downward angle. Evading their fire is easy. The huge battleship looms before you as you bank hard and open fire with your M2 Browning machine guns. The bullets whiz through the air, decorating the battleship's deck with tiny holes. You can see your shots are having a deadly effect on the enemy gun crew.

Your fellow Hellcat pilots follow your lead. Waves of fighters attack the Japanese battleship, coming in just above the waves and peppering the deck with machine gun fire. Soon, all of the ship's antiaircraft guns are destroyed.

"The path is clear," Thomas announces. "Bring on the bombers!"

Over the next several hours, the battle rages on. The Allies pummel the *Yamato* with bombs and torpedoes. No Japanese air support ever arrives. The battleship is dead in the water. You circle the skies as it begins to sink. You realize that this moment marks the unofficial end of the Japanese navy. You'd love to get one last look at the *Yamato* before it goes down. Think of the great story it would make.

To return to your carrier, turn to page 88.

To do a quick fly-over before returning, turn to page 100.

You try to use your Hellcat's speed to your advantage. You climb to more than 10,000 feet. "Going in!" you say over the radio.

As you dive your Hellcat slices through the air at nearly 400 miles per hour. The *Yamato* starts out as a small dot on the ocean surface below. But at that speed, it grows bigger by the second. You let one of your unguided Tiny Tim rockets fly. Then you open fire with your M2 Browning machine guns.

antiaircraft guns at Okinawa, July 1945

But you're not the only one opening fire. You can see several of the antiaircraft guns swinging around to target you. You realize that you're a sitting duck up here. You're going too fast to evade the fire. And the enemy guns' range is far greater than yours. They're going to shoot you out of the sky before you can do any real damage.

To break off the attack, turn to page 86.

To carry on in hopes of taking out one of the enemy guns, turn to page 95.

Japanese pilots often use suicide attacks against Allied ships. But that's not a part of your handbook. Your attack is doomed, so you pull back as hard as you can, banking left. You need to get out of range, and fast.

But it's too late. One of the antiaircraft guns opens fire. Bullets tear through your Hellcat's tail section and one of your wings. You do all you can to control it, but the damage is too great. All you can do is glide the wounded plane closer to the range of the Allied fleet.

Finally, you have no choice but to bail. You force the plane's bubbled window up to open it. Then you unclip your seatbelt and let the wind carry you out of the plane.

Your parachute opens and floats you gently down to the waters of the Pacific below. You cringe as your Hellcat crashes into the ocean, and watch helplessly as it sinks under the waves.

Eventually a rescue boat picks you up. You watch the rest of the battle from there. Your fellow pilots use low attacks to take out the *Yamato*'s guns. Then the bombers do the rest. The *Yamato* never has a chance. The great ship joins your Hellcat on the ocean floor.

Turn to page 99.

Your mission is accomplished. It's time to get back to your carrier. You're eager to see how the battle there is coming.

As you turn and fly away, an enormous blast shakes your plane. You look back. The *Yamato* has exploded! A huge mushroom-shaped cloud rises up from the wreckage. The fires must have reached its ammunition stores. You take a deep breath. If you'd gone in for a closer look, you'd have been caught in the blast. You just hope nobody else made that mistake.

88

Turn to page 97.

You're not about to let your best friend down. You bank hard to your right. Gordon is leading the chase away from the destroyer and the rest of the battle group. But the Zeros are gaining ground. It's only a matter of time before they shoot him down.

As Gordon and the Japanese pilots duck and weave, you catch them. Again, you open fire. Direct hit! One of the Zeros goes down. The other two quickly break off their pursuit.

Japanese planes had red circles painted on the wings.
The circles represented the rising sun on Japan's flag.

Turn the page.

"What are you doing?" Gordon shouts angrily.

"Saving your behind," you answer, banking around to re-engage. But before you can add anything more, you see a sight that makes your blood run cold. The destroyer that you were protecting has been hit. One of the enemy Zeros has slammed into its bridge. Flames rise and the big ship begins to lean to one side.

The ship is damaged beyond repair. You know that it will sink here, and you can't guess how many lives will be lost.

You know you'll have nightmares about that destroyer for the rest of your life. But there's no time to stop now. The battle has just begun. Maybe you can find some way to make up for your terrible mistake.

THE END

To follow another path, turn to page 9.

To read the conclusion, turn to page 103.

You don't need to think twice. Protecting the fleet is your top priority. You bank hard to the right, using the Corsair's speed to close the distance to the Zeros. You can see the ship's antiaircraft guns blazing. But destroyers are built to fight mainly submarines and surface ships. The Zeros zip left and right, staying clear of the fire.

Their evasive maneuvers slow them down though. Soon you're within range. You open fire with your machine guns. A stream of bullets tears into the tail section of an enemy plane. But you don't even pause to watch it go down. The other plane is diving. It's only a few dozen feet off the surface, and it's closing fast. You don't have a chance to get it. It's going to ram right into the ship!

91

Turn the page.

But before it does, the Zero explodes in a ball of flames.

"Got him!" says Gordon over the radio.

You breathe a sigh of relief. You can't wait to hear Gordon tell the story of how he ditched the Zeros chasing him. But that will have to wait.

"More Zeros coming in from the north," Gordon says.

You've done your job. That destroyer is still afloat because of your actions. But the enemy isn't letting up, and you have no time to celebrate.

92

"Let's go," you answer as you turn to engage the next enemy.

Turn to page 97.

You've only got one chance to bring down this enemy plane, and you're going to take it. You go full speed toward the Ki-45. Soon you're almost on top of it. You can't help but wonder what the enemy pilot thinks of this crazy maneuver.

CRUNCH! Your propeller blades tear into the Ki-45's tail, slicing it completely off of the enemy aircraft!

"Gotcha!" you shout. You can see that part of your propeller blade is missing. But your Corsair is still handling like a champ. That's something that your enemy can't say.

"What was that?" you hear over the radio. It's Gordon. "I just shot mine down the easy way."

"Guns jammed," you answer. "Figure I ought to get some sort of medal for that move."

"OK hero. You ready to get back to battle?"

Turn the page.

"I'll have to stop off for a fresh ride, but you know I'll be back!" you say, flashing him a thumbs-up out the window.

With that, it's back to your carrier. There, the crew can fix this plane while you return to battle in a new one. Already the ship is buzzing about your amazing kill. But you just want to get back in the air.

94

Turn to page 97.

You've got to take out those guns to clear the way for the Allied bombers. So it's full speed ahead. With your machine guns blazing, you continue your dive.

The *Yamato* opens fire. You do all you can to evade the stream of bullets. But at this speed, there's little maneuvering you can do. Bullets tear into one of your wings. You lose control of the plane, which begins to spin.

You're doomed. You try to open the plane's window to bail. But you never get the chance. Another stream of bullets tears into the Hellcat, hitting your fuel tanks. Luckily for you, you're unconscious before your plane turns into a giant fireball, then crashes into the sea. You're another victim of the bloody Battle of Okinawa.

95

THE END

To follow another path, turn to page 9.

To read the conclusion, turn to page 103.

With your guns jammed, you decide it's time to break off your pursuit. Better to get back to the carrier and let the crew get your Corsair back in working shape.

"What's the problem, Captain?" says your commanding officer after you land.

"Guns jammed. Had to come back."

"We're short on planes," he says. "Why don't you rest. Maybe we'll get you back up tomorrow."

You know better than to argue. The battle rages on around you. But your part in it is done, at least for today.

96

Turn to page 99.

The fighting continues through the day. Both sides suffer losses. The Japanese kamikaze attacks take out several Allied ships. But in the end, the Japanese losses are far greater. The *Yamato* has been destroyed, as have countless aircraft. And the Allies have taken a clear advantage in the battle.

But it's far from over.

The Battle of Okinawa was the bloodiest battle fought on the Pacific front. It was fought on land, at sea, and in the air.

Turn the page.

The fight stretches on for several more months, officially lasting for 82 days. You fly one successful mission after the next, doing all you can to support the troops on the ground.

In the end, the Allies win Okinawa. But the losses on both sides are staggering. Nearly all of the *Yamato*'s crew was lost. In total, more than 12,000 Americans lost their lives, and around 70,000 Japanese soldiers were killed. Between 100,000 and 150,000 Okinawan civilians died, caught up in the fighting. You are lucky to have survived the bloody Battle of Okinawa.

THE END

To follow another path, turn to page 9.

To read the conclusion, turn to page 103.

That night your fellow pilots are all talking about their day. The fighting was bloody on both sides. Several of your good friends were shot down, and a few didn't make it back. But the Japanese were hit far worse.

"I got two," brags Frank.

"Just one for me," says Gordon.

You slip quietly out of the room, hoping nobody sees. You didn't score a single kill. The Battle of Okinawa will stretch on for months. You hope that you'll be able to prove yourself next time.

99

THE END

To follow another path, turn to page 9.

To read the conclusion, turn to page 103.

This is history in the making, and you're right here to see it.

"Battle's over," says Thomas over the radio. "Let's head back."

"Right behind you. Just gotta take one last look," you answer.

You bring your plane down and set course for a quick flyby. As you approach you see what bad shape the *Yamato* is in. Half of the ship is underwater. Much of the rest is on fire.

You're about to pull up and head back when it happens. The *Yamato* explodes. The blast is so huge and so loud that it is heard more than 100 miles away. Your fellow pilots will talk about the blast and your death in the same breath.

THE END

To follow another path, turn to page 9.

To read the conclusion, turn to page 103.

Only 269 of the *Yamato*'s 3,000-man crew survived the ship's explosion.

Germany's capital city, Berlin, was captured on April 30, 1945.

5
WAR'S END

World War II raged across Europe and the Pacific Ocean for six years. The exact number of casualties suffered will never be known, although estimates range between 60 million and 85 million military and civilian deaths. What we do know is that it was the bloodiest war in history.

Before the Battle of Stalingrad, the German army had seemed almost unstoppable. But when the Soviets defeated the famous German 6th Army, everything changed. The Germans had spent too many resources in the failed attempt to capture the city. Their forces were spread too thin. When the Allies attacked from the west, the Germans were unable to hold their ground.

The Allies stormed the beach at Normandy, France, in June 1944. By the winter of that year, the German army was forced to retreat back to their border. Hitler and his leaders planned a last desperate offensive to break the Allied line in two at the Battle of the Bulge. The tactic nearly succeeded, but in the end, the Allies won.

By April 1945 the German capital of Berlin was surrounded. Germany had no choice but to surrender. Their leader, Adolf Hitler, took his own life, rather than be captured.

The battle in the Pacific carried on, however. At Okinawa the Allies finally took control of the valuable Ryuku Islands in June 1945. The plan was to use the islands as a staging point for an invasion of the Japanese mainland. It was shaping up to be the biggest and deadliest battle in the entire war.

But the invasion never happened. In August 1945 the United States military unleashed a new weapon of terrible power—the atomic bomb. The first bomb was dropped on Hiroshima, Japan, on August 6. Nagasaki was bombed three days later. Both cities were utterly destroyed. Hundreds of thousands of people were killed.

Japan announced its surrender less than a week later. On September 2 Japan's surrender became official. World War II was finally over.

The blast from the atomic bomb destroyed 6 square miles of Hiroshima.

TIMELINE

July 7, 1939—Japan invades China, which begins the war in the Pacific.

September 1, 1939—World War II officially begins in Europe when German forces invade Poland. Great Britain and France enter the war to protect Poland.

September 27, 1940—Japan, Germany, and Italy join forces to become the Axis nations.

June–November 1941—The Axis attacks the Soviet Union.

December 7, 1941—Japanese planes bomb Pearl Harbor, Hawaii. The United States enters the war to fight with the Allied forces.

August 1942—The Battle of Stalingrad begins. German aircraft bomb the city heavily before the German 6th Army moves in.

November 1942–February 1943—The Soviet army launches Operation Uranus. They break through the Axis lines north and south of Stalingrad, surrounding the Germans. Eventually Germany's 6th Army surrenders.

July 25, 1943—Italian leader Benito Mussolini is overthrown. The new government surrenders to the Allies.

June 6, 1944—The Allies storm the beaches of Normandy in France, forcing the Germans to fight the war on two fronts.

August 25, 1944—Allied troops reach Paris, France.

October 20, 1944—Allied troops land in the Philippines.

December 16, 1944—The Germans launch a surprise attack on the Allied line at the Battle of the Bulge. It is unsuccessful and they are forced to retreat.

April 1945—The Battle of Okinawa begins as Allied forces invade the Ryuku Islands.

April 30, 1945—Berlin is surrounded. Nazi leader Adolf Hitler commits suicide.

May 7, 1945—Germany surrenders, ending the war in Europe.

May 1945—The Allies take control of Okinawa and prepare to invade Japan.

August 6, 1945—A U.S. plane drops an atomic bomb on the Japanese city of Hiroshima. The blast destroys more than 6 square miles of the city.

August 9, 1945—A second atomic bomb is dropped on Nagasaki. Between the two cities, more than 120,000 people are killed from the blasts. Thousands more die from radiation poisoning and other injuries.

September 2, 1945—The Japanese surrender becomes official, six years and one day after the beginning of the war.

OTHER PATHS TO EXPLORE

In this book, you've explored several key battles from the perspectives of the men who fought them. But perspectives in history are as varied as the people who lived it. You can explore other paths on your own to learn more about World War II. Seeing history from many points of view is a key to understanding it.

Here are some ideas for other World War II points of view to explore:

+ Imagine what life might have been like as a Jewish person in Germany or a Nazi-controlled country. How would you survive in a land whose leaders wanted you dead? (Integration of Knowledge and Ideas)

+ Think about what it might have been like as a resident of Hiroshima when that first atomic bomb fell. How terrifying would it have been? What would you have thought of the Americans for dropping it? (Key Ideas and Details)

+ Imagine yourself as a former German soldier after the war. How would you feel about the fall of Nazi Germany? (Integration of Knowledge and Ideas)

READ MORE

Benoit, Peter. *Big Battles of World War II.*
New York: Children's Press, 2014.

Cooke, Tim. *World War II on the Front Lines.*
North Mankato, Minn.: Capstone Press, 2014.

Gitlin, Marty. *World War II on the Home Front:
An Interactive History Adventure.* Mankato, Minn.:
Capstone Press, 2012.

INTERNET SITES

Use FactHound to find Internet sites related to this book.
All of the sites on FactHound have been researched by
our staff.

Here's all you do:
Visit *www.facthound.com*
Type in this code: 9781491421529

GLOSSARY

artillery (ar-TI-luhr-ee)—cannons and other large guns used during battles

bank (BANGK)—to tilt an airplane sideways when turning

battalion (buh-TAL-yuhn)—a group of soldiers

battery (BA-tuh-ree)—a group of heavy guns that are all used together

bayonet (BAY-uh-net)—a long metal blade attached to the end of a rifle

civilian (si-VIL-yuhn)—a person who is not in the military

debris (duh-BREE)—the scattered pieces of something that has been broken or destroyed

elite (i-LEET)—a group of people who have special advantages or talents

entrenched (en-TRENCH-d)—in a strong position that cannot easily be changed

fleet (FLEET)—a group of warships under one command

foxhole (FOX-hohl)—a hole dug for a soldier to sit or lie in for protection

howitzer (HOU-uht-sur)—a cannon that shoots explosive shells long distances

invasion (in-VEY-zhuhn)—when a country's military forces enter another country to take it over

kamikaze (kah-mi-KAH-zee)—a Japanese pilot during World War II who would purposely crash his plane into a target, resulting in his own death

magazine (MAG-uh-zeen)—a metal or plastic case that holds bullets and fits inside a gun

Panzer (PAN-zur)—a German tank of World War II

prefecture (pre-FECT-shure)—an area of a town or city governed by a governor

truce (TROOS)—a temporary agreement to stop fighting

BIBLIOGRAPHY

Bishop, Chris, ed. *The Encyclopedia of Weapons of World War II.* New York: MetroBooks, 2002.

Bruning, John R. *The Battle of the Bulge: The Photographic History of an American Triumph.* Minneapolis: MBI Pub. Co. and Zenith Press, 2009.

Graff, Cory. *F6F Hellcat at War.* Minneapolis: MBI Publishing Company, 2009.

Gregory, Don A., and Wilhelm R. Gehlen, eds. *Two Soldiers, Two Lost Fronts: German War Diaries of the Stalingrad and North Africa Campaigns.* Philadelphia: Casemate, 2009.

Holmes, Richard, ed. *The Hutchinson Atlas of Battle Plans: Before and After.* Chicago: Fitzroy Dearborn Publishers, 1999.

Kennedy, Maxwell Taylor. *Danger's Hour: The Story of the USS Bunker Hill and the Kamikaze Pilot Who Crippled Her.* New York: Simon & Schuster, 2008.

Leckie, Robert. *Okinawa: The Last Battle of World War II.* New York: Viking, 1995.

Martel, Gordon, ed. *Twentieth-Century War and Conflict: A Concise Encyclopedia.* Chichester, West Sussex: John Wiley & Sons Ltd, 2014.

Münch, Karlheinz. *The Combat History of German Heavy Anti-Tank Unit 653 in World War II.* Mechanicsburg, Pa.: Stackpole Books, 2005.

Suermondt, Jan. *Infantry Weapons of World War II.* Minneapolis: Chartwell Books, 2012.

Walsh, Stephen. *Stalingrad: The Infernal Cauldron, 1942–1943.* New York: Thomas Dunne Books, 2000.

INDEX

AT BATTLE IN WORLD WAR II

AN INTERACTIVE BATTLEFIELD ADVENTURE

by Matt Doeden

3 STORY PATHS

46 CHOICES

17 ENDINGS

YOU CHOOSE
BOOKS